SAN FRANCISCO
FROM THE AIR

Featuring the Photography of Neil Sutherland and Julian Essam

CLB 1433
© 1987 Illustrations and text: Colour Library Books Ltd.,
  Guildford, Surrey, England.
Text filmsetting by Acesetters Ltd., Richmond, Surrey, England.
All rights reserved.
Published 1987 by Crescent Books, distributed by Crown Publishers, Inc.
Printed and bound in Barcelona, Spain by Cronion, S.A.
ISBN 0 517 49053 6
h g f e d c b a

Dep.Leg. B-2.258-86

SAN FRANCISCO
FROM THE AIR

Text by
Bill Harris

CRESCENT BOOKS
NEW YORK

Unlike many of the other great cities of the world, people were looking at San Francisco from above long before anyone ever saw it from the air. The earliest settlers climbed the steep trail to the top of "the Hill of Golden Promise" to get a better look at their new home and the neighborhood around it. In the mid 19th century, it became the best neighborhood in the city, and though the railroad magnates and Bonanza Kings who built fancy mansions there didn't mind its original name, the folks they looked down upon changed it to "Nob Hill."

Maybe it was because the tops of San Francisco's hills had become symbols of the rich and powerful that the urge to fly hit San Franciscans a little bit harder than other Americans. Possibly it was because they had a better opportunity than most to preview the experience. Though Wilbur and Orville Wright were Americans, their countrymen didn't pay much attention to them when they announced that they had invented an air machine and had actually flown one. They had to take their idea to Europe, where the Germans, French and British not only accepted them, but spent fortunes establishing companies to build heavier-than-air flying machines. It wasn't until 1909, nearly six years after the Wrights had flown over the beach at Kitty Hawk, N.C., that Americans began to notice them. Americans weren't too fascinated by gas-filled airships, either. They had seen balloonists at county fairs and had long since decided that, though it was a cute trick, a country dedicated to forward progress didn't have much use for something that just went up and down.

It took a San Franciscan to demonstrate that they were probably wrong. In the early years of the 20th century, about the same time the Wright Brothers were putting wings on motorbikes and Professor Samuel Langley was eating up a $50,000 Federal grant trying to devise a flying "aerodrome," Dr. August Greth of San Francisco announced that he had invented a dirigible that could be navigated and take you someplace besides up and down. His ship, along with the 1904 *California Arrow*, built by Captain Tom Baldwin and powered by a modified motorcycle engine designed by Glenn Curtiss, is generally considered the first successful airship built by an American.

What Greth had built was not a dirigible, but rather what his detractors said it was: an old fashioned balloon with a different shape. But though it looked more like a fish than a lightbulb, it could be maneuvered without relying on gusts of wind.

Dirigibles, on the other hand, were already a reality. A dirigible is a cigar-shaped balloon that has a rigid frame supporting gas-filled cells inside. It was invented by Count Ferdinand von Zeppelin, who had been sent to America during the Civil War as a military advisor. The Americans had used captive balloons as observation posts and the idea fascinated the Count. When he retired, he went to work in earnest and by 1900 he had already flown passengers between Berlin and Lake Constance.

Nearly 30 years later, in 1929, literally all of San Francisco was outdoors, shielding its eyes from the sun for a better look at the *Graf Zeppelin* on its way to Los Angeles after a flight from Tokyo. The Count's heirs obviously knew the value of slightly deviating a flight plan for public relations. The *Graf Zeppelin* was just a year old that day. The flight was part of an around-the-world cruise. She had a crew of 41 and a passenger list of 20.

Obviously, the passengers were well-treated. Not only did they get a dramatic view of San Francisco from the air, but they were able to do it from an over-stuffed couch through curtained windows that could be kept open in flight. Some could have been on the promenade deck where the windows were set at an angle that allowed for better views. Some may have been lingering over lunch, which was being catered by the finest restaurant in Tokyo. (For the next leg of their trip, from Los Angeles to Lakehurst, New Jersey, their meals would be provided by chefs from the Biltmore Hotel.)

Some of the passengers aboard the *Graf Zeppelin* that day might even have decided to stay in bed. Every berth on board had a view. Every berth also had a button next to it that would produce your favorite cocktail. Another would summon a waiter in case you wanted breakfast, lunch and dinner in bed. Being German, they had very strict rules about hours, and if you pushed the button after ten in the morning, you'd get lunch, like it or not. But you could get a drink any time you pushed that other button.

The Zeppelin had a lot of rules that needed to be followed strictly. The most important of them was that smoking was not allowed except in a specially-built room. Even the lighting of matches was forbidden.

An unfortunate rule, which was imposed by an international agreement, and not unilaterally by the German government, was that cameras had to be turned over to the purser. It was forbidden to take pictures of any of the countries the airship was flying over. It was also forbidden to throw anything out of the windows.

But the amenities more than made up for the inconveniences. The murals in the dining room were colorful representations of the airship on a voyage to South America. The writing room was decorated with original paintings tracing the development of postal service from Chinese messengers to the *Graf Zeppelin* itself, the latter painting being near the pneumatic tube that sped your letters and postcards right to the mailroom.

The promenade, with its 45-degree windows, had carpeted floors and cushioned seats for the comfort of passengers who spent hours watching the world go by a couple of hundred feet below them. If there were joggers among them, the promenade encircled the entire part of the airship's gondola, which allowed about 200 feet of running space.

The smoking room, a pressurized, 15-foot cabin, also featured a bar, whose custodian was the only person on board permitted to carry matches. But he preferred that you lit your cigarettes with his flameless lighter, which eventually became useful in automobiles. The bartender also had the responsibility of making sure no one went through the airlock without first leaving their cigarettes and cigars behind. Since the room and the bar stayed open until three in the morning, it seems likely that the bartender must have had his hands full in the wee hours with people who wanted to visit the promenade for a breath of fresh air and a late-night cigar.

The only complaint ever heard from a *Graf Zeppelin* passenger was that the airship didn't have a piano aboard. When the same company built the *Hindenburg* in 1936, they corrected the oversight.

When the great *Graf Zeppelin* flew over San Francisco in 1929, everybody agreed that airplanes would never duplicate the luxury of an airship and that the future of trans-ocean travel by air clearly belonged to the big dirigibles. But from the beginning, the only value of air travel, as Americans saw it, was to get there faster. Comfort was nice, but time, after all, is money.

Until the mid-1930s, the only airplane service across the Atlantic was a mail plane that flew between West Africa and Brazil. Nobody had figured out how to fly across the Pacific with a heavier-than-air machine.

The man who finally did figure it out was Juan Trippe, whose Pan American Airline had begun flying to Cuba and other Central and South American destinations in 1927. By 1930, their planes were flying from Brownsville, Texas and Miami, Florida as far down the Pacific coast as Santiago, Chile. Their pilots were becoming the most experienced in the world at flying long distances and navigating water routes. Aircraft designers were better able to work out the problems they encountered and, in 1931, Pan Am sent out a challenge to build an airplane that could fly a 300-pound mailbag 2,500 miles non-stop.

Two companies took up the challenge, Sikorsky and G.L. Martin. The Sikorsky plane, the S-42, was the biggest airplane built for an American carrier up to that time. It could carry a 300-pound mailbag. It could also carry 32 passengers over shorter distances. Pan Am ordered three of them. Martin came up with the M-130, a four-engine flying boat, slightly smaller than the S-42, but capable of carrying 35 passengers. Pan Am ordered three of those, too. When it was decided to use the M-130 for trans-Pacific service, it was christened the "Pan American Clipper" in honor of the clipper ships that once followed the same route.

The route began in San Francisco when the first flying boat, *China Clipper*, left the airport at Alameda in the East Bay area on November 22, 1935. It arrived in Manila seven days later with a 1,837-pound mailbag aboard.

But though that represents the beginnings of an important chapter in the history of aviation in America, it also marked the end of another story.

The *China Clipper* had been flying for about a year on the 2,500-mile round trip run between Miami and the U.S. Virgin

Islands. In the spring of 1935, it was taken to its San Francisco base, from where it began making test flights up and down the coast. But Manila was 8,200 miles away. The range of the plane was 2,500 miles. Before the trip could be made, it was necessary to establish bases enroute. Two obvious places were Wake Island and Midway Island. But neither island had any of the raw materials necessary to either build an airport or to sustain the people who would run it.

Much of the work was done in San Francisco. Two complete prefabricated villages were constructed, and all the materials needed for the bases, from dynamite to aviation fuel, were assembled on a San Francisco dock and loaded aboard a ship, which left the harbor on March 27, eight months before the plane was scheduled to leave. One hundred and eighteen technicians and construction workers were also on board. The Wake and Midway facilities were built simultaneously, and a former military facility at Guam was rebuilt before they called the job finished. Each of the bases was equipped with sea-going launches with a thousand-mile range; they were designed to handle any emergency, including refueling, and if all else failed they could tow a flying boat back to base.

Once the first trip had been made, the rest seemed easy. After that, a regular schedule of one flight a week began when the *Hawaii Clipper* left Alameda bound for Manila with seven paying passengers aboard on October 21, 1936. The fare was $360 one-way to Honolulu, $799 to Manila. More than 1,100 people tried to buy tickets for the seven seats. The trip took six days, 60 hours of which were in the air. The airline had decided against flying any major portion of the trip at night, when pilots couldn't see turbulence-producing cumulo-nimbus clouds. Night landings were also difficult, so the schedule was arranged to eliminate them and hotel facilities were provided for overnight stops at each of the ports of call. The final leg from Guam began at two in the morning to insure arrival in Manila before sunset. A long and arduous trip, to be sure, but it took more than three times as long by ship.

Besides, everyone agreed it was much more fun to fly over the Golden Gate Bridge than to sail under it.

And the airplane, though not as luxurious as a Zeppelin, nor as comfortable as a cruise ship, was quite the best thing in the air. The most common plane in use back in 1936 was the Boeing 247, which cost an airline $75,000. The Martin M-130 cost $417,201. The interior was divided into separate cabins, one of which was a dining room where passengers shared a long table and ate from china plates. The other two cabins were designed to look like the lounges on transcontinental trains. Sleeping berths were also included, even though schedules kept flying time down to about six hours a day.

Flight stewards operated from a four-foot square galley, from which passengers were encouraged to help themselves to ice and fresh water, as well as cotton ear plugs and air-sickness bags. The stewards would provide you with hot coffee or chocolate, sandwiches or fresh fruit. They also dispensed aspirin, smelling salts, Dramamine and sugar tablets free of charge. But cigarettes, mineral water and alcohol cost extra.

They had a wine list, too. But as one British passenger pointed out as he ordered his Scotch and soda, wine in those days was considered fit only for banquets and foreigners. Tipping was strictly forbidden, though it had been encouraged on steamships and trains. All things considered, it was an experience to write home about. As the British traveler said in his postcard home, the trip across the Pacific in a flying boat was very much like being in a comfortable, friendly club.

But if San Francisco was part of the history of establishing air connections between North America and the Far East, it was also where the first air link with the folks back East was established. In 1926, a Pacific Northwest lumberman named Bill Boeing made a bid for carrying air mail from San Francisco to Chicago. His new company, Boeing Air Transport, used a fast little plane he was turning out in a converted boatyard up in Seattle. The Boeing 40-A could cruise at 125 miles an hour with 1,200 pounds of mail, two passengers and the pilot. He operated daily round trips with a flight leaving San Francisco at 6:00 a.m. and another westbound from Chicago at 7:50 a.m. The trip took about 24 hours. The one-way fare was $200. He also scheduled stops along the way in Nevada, Utah, Wyoming, Nebraska and Iowa.

The comfort of larger planes eventually made his 40-A obsolete. Transcontinental Air Transport, which merged with Western Air a few years later and became TWA, had introduced Ford Trimotors to the West Coast. Not only did the plane have comfortable seats but it sported reading lights, luggage racks and a toilet. Bill Boeing went back to Seattle to build better airplanes.

Another man out of the Northwest arrived in San Francisco in 1925 with an idea about flying in another direction. He was Vern Gorst, who operated a network of bus routes in Oregon. Gorst was fascinated by the idea of aviation and, flying from Crissy Field in San Francisco, went as far north as British Columbia then south to the Mexican border to map north-south airmail routes. He eventually served those routes and the cities along them, including San Francisco, using a new plane developed by Californian Claude Ryan, who had earned his reputation converting World War I-surplus bi-planes into planes that could carry four passengers plus the pilot. He had flown them on a regular schedule between Los Angeles and San Diego, making him, in 1925, the first operator of a passenger air service in the United States.

Thanks to Gorst, he went out of the airline business and, like Bill Boeing, concentrated on airplane building. The first ten he built became the workhorses of Vern Gorst's Pacific Air Transport Company, which began carrying mail and passengers between Los Angeles and Seattle in 1926. The passengers rode with the mailbags and paid $132 for the privilege. Gorst himself set up his headquarters in a cheap hotel on San Francisco's Mission Street. But he was never sorry he got out of the bus business. The airline business turned out fairly well. We know it as United Airlines today.

The airlines that made aviation history in the San Francisco area serve it well today. San Francisco International Airport is one of America's ten busiest, with well over 400,000 takeoffs and landings a year. The lucky passengers aboard those planes see much more than those forty-niners who climbed to the top of Nob Hill to have a look at San Francisco from above. Most get a chance to see San Francisco from the air.

Looking north from San Francisco's Seacliff district and China Beach towards Baker Beach in the San Francisco Presidio and Golden Gate Bridge.

Dubbed the "Path of Gold", Market Street (facing page) is a major transit corridor for the San Francisco Municipal Railway, which operates the city's trademark cable cars as well as a fleet of buses, streetcars and trolley coaches. The system copes with over 700,000 riders on an average weekday, and was the first transportation system in the U.S. to be owned and operated by the city. Above: a view of the Marina District, with the Golden Gate Bridge beyond. Overleaf: the Port of San Francisco (left) is a natural, deepwater port and extends for 7.5 miles along the western shore of San Francisco, from the Hyde Street Pier on the north to Hunters Point on the south. Today, the northern waterfront (shown) contains many non-maritime commercial developments, including the shops and restaurants of Pier 39, the Cannery, Ghirardelli Square, the Anchorage and Fisherman's Wharf, as well as a commercial fishing hub and the only exclusive passenger terminal in the Bay Area. Right: one of the new Marine developments in Marin County.

Above: looking east toward the Port of Oakland, with its vast container shipping facilities and (to the right) NAS Alameda. Facing page: to the south of the Ferry Building, the Port of San Francisco has opened up a 1,600-foot stretch of shoreline formerly hidden by Piers 14 to 22. Financial District workers are drawn to the Embarcadero Waterfront Promenade to lunch, jog, fish, bask in the sun and sea-gaze. Its basic feature is a 1,200-foot-long, granite-faced "bench" five feet from the water's edge with walkways on different elevations at either side. Overleaf: just how many hills San Francisco covers is a moot question – enough, certainly, to provide a whole succession of spectacular views. Some sources list upward of 40. The main ones – Nob, Russian, Telegraph, Rincon, Twin Peaks, Mount Davidson and Lone Mountain, clearly earned it the Roman sobriquet, "City of Seven Hills."

Previous pages: (left) a nautical wonderland unfolds... Pier 39, which offers many fine restaurants with international cuisine, a collection of specialty shops, the San Francisco Experience Theatre and continuous free street entertainment by jugglers, mime artists and musicians. Beyond is Pier 41, embarkation point for bay cruises and Alcatraz Island tours, the sailing schooner *Balclutha*, world-famous Fisherman's Wharf and the historic ships collection at Hyde Street Pier. Honeycombed with picturesque alleys, stairways and terraced gardens, Telegraph Hill (right) was named after a semaphore which was once used to signal the approach of ships through the Golden Gate. The complex at the base of the hill is world headquarters of Levi Strauss & Co. Above: James Lick Freeway (named for one of the city's early benefactors) serpentines through light industrial area. Facing page: the magnificent Golden Gate Bridge, one of the longest single-span suspension bridges in the world. Overleaf: Union Square, the green oasis in the foreground, is synonymous with downtown. The Westin St. Francis Hotel is situated on the Square's western edge. The scene of pro-Union demonstrations during the 1860s, the Square is adorned by a slender shaft commemorating Admiral Dewey's victory in Manila Bay. Underneath is the nation's first underground parking garage.

Previous pages: the cluster of red-brick buildings (right) at the base of Telegraph Hill is world headquarters for Levi Strauss & Co., one of the city's oldest and best known firms. Marina Boulevard, (left) lined with Mediterranean-like villas with price tags in the region of $1,000,000, affords a close-up prospect of the St. Francis Yacht Harbor and the bay beyond. Above: portions of the forested site of the Presidio of San Francisco, which are components of the Golden Gate National Recreation Area, the largest urban park in the world and most popular of the U.S. National Parks. Known in some quarters as the "gilded ghetto", Chinatown (facing page) is the largest community of its kind outside Asia. Overleaf: (left) the golden gateway to the Pacific. Once a workaday world of small, service industries, the city's South of Market precinct (right, foreground) has been targeted by developers for a number of highrise projects.

27

Coit Tower (previous pages), the central fluted cylinder, was built as a monument to San Francisco's volunteer firemen in 1933. Lillie Hitchcock Coit, an honorary member of Knickerbocker Number Five Fire Company, left a $100,000 bequest from her estate to fund the construction. An elevator to the tower's 210-foot observation platform operates daily. Nob Hill (above), the posh purlieu of Gold Rush and railroad barons during the 1870s, was once dubbed the "hill of palaces" by Robert Louis Stevenson. The main artery, California Street, plunges to Financial District, while the San Francisco-Oakland Bay Bridge looms in the background. Facing page: the southern approach of the Golden Gate Bridge narrows to six lanes on the main span. The historic brick bastion of Fort Point, which opened in 1861 and was declared a National Historic Site in 1970, slumbers beneath an arch. Overleaf: (left) the Palace of Fine Arts, a monumental, 70-year-old Greco-Romanesque rotunda with Corinthian colonnades, which was reconstructed at a cost of $8 million in 1967. The red-roofed buildings are part of the 1,500-acre Presidio of San Francisco, headquarters for the U.S. Sixth Army. (Right) gull's-eye view of San Francisco's northern waterfront, which includes piers of Fort Mason Center, the semi-circle of Aquatic Park lagoon and the commercial shipping hub beyond.

Previous pages: the University of San Francisco (right) was founded in 1855; the church in the foreground is that of St. Ignatius. Columbus Avenue (left), which bisects the city's North Beach and Chinatown neighborhoods, is lined with *trattorias*, import shops and coffee houses. It was the great explorer John Fremont who named the city's portal (above) on the Pacific, the Golden Gate... "The bay of San Francisco has been celebrated from the time of its first discovery as one of the finest in the world. It rises into an importance far above that of a mere harbor... its latitudinal position is that of Lisbon, its climate that of Southern Italy, settlements attest to its healthfulness, bold shores and mountains give it grandeur, the extent and fertility of its dependent country give it great resources for agriculture, commerce and population... To this gate I gave the name Chysopylae or Golden Gate." The outer Richmond District (facing page), flanked by the Golden Gate, the Pacific Ocean and Golden Gate Park, is an area of tidy rowhouses. In the background lies a forested area, formerly the grounds of the Adolph Sutro estate. Just offshore are the abrupt outlines of Seal Rocks. Overleaf: during the early part of this century, San Francisco Bay (left) harbored the world's largest ferry fleet. Today the city and the North Bay are served by 17 ferries sailing under the ensigns of the Golden Gate Bridge District, the Red & White Fleet and the Blue & Gold Fleet. Some 37,000,000 vehicles cross the Golden Gate Bridge (right) annually. The "bridge that couldn't be built" according to skeptics of Joseph Strauss' visionary plan, celebrates its 50th anniversary in May, 1987.

Previous pages: nowadays, San Francisco's Ferry Building (lower right hand corner) is dwarfed by dozens of downtown highrises.
Above: one of the city's oldest and most prestigious yacht clubs, the St. Francis, hugs the northern waterfront of San Francisco Bay.
Facing page: the 8.5-acre, $135 million Embarcadero Center complex, which features the innovative Hyatt Regency hotel, an outdoor stage and 175 shops and restaurants.

Previous pages: (left) skyscrapers in the financial district are capped by everything from the rooftop gardens on the Shaklee Building to the pointed crown of the Transamerica Pyramid. Developed on the site of the 1915 Panama Pacific International Exposition, the Marina District (right) is bracketed on the west by the Palace of Fine Arts, which houses the Exploratorium, and on the east by Fort Mason Center, a lively arts and recreation community offering over 1,000 events monthly. Above: Alcatraz, where tour boats dock to the north of the main cell block at center right. The prison workshops stand left foreground. Facing page: Oakland Bay Bridge, with the attractive downtown area beyond. Overleaf: some 14,000 residential examples of Victorian architecture remain part of the urban landscape in San Francisco. There are three basic designs – Italianate, Queen Anne and Stick, or Eastlake – all of which are represented in this panorama of the Mission District near San Francisco General Hospital.

Above: the St. Francis Yacht Harbor, with the Marina Green, Gas House Cove, Fort Mason (headquarters of the Golden Gate National Recreation Area), and the crescent pier of Aquatic Park beyond. The park at center is George R. Moscone Recreation Center. San Francisco has a marvellous variety of modern architecture (facing page) with new designs always underway. Overleaf: San Francisco's Civic Center (left), landmarked by domed City Hall and surrounded by the Performing Arts Center, Federal and State Office Buildings, Public Library and Civic Auditorium. Beneath the plaza is Brooks (exhibition) Hall. (Right) looking north up (from left) Polk, Larking and Hyde streets toward Aquatic Park, Ghirardelli Square and Hyde Street Pier, with Alcatraz in the background.

Point Lobos Avenue (above) swoops through Sutro Heights past the Cliff House and along San Francisco's Ocean Beach, where it becomes the Great Highway. Facing page: Sidney Walton Park, framed on three sides by the apartment towers and townhouses of the Golden Gateway Center. Overleaf: the view west from Battery Street, looking up from Broadway (which enters the tunnel center right), Vallejo and Green streets. The panorama takes in, from the left, Nob Hill, Russian Hill and (right foreground) Telegraph Hill.

Above: Geary Boulevard sweeps east through San Francisco's Western Addition, past Japantown and St. Mary's Cathedral to the city's shopping and financial district. Facing page: the Marina District. Overleaf: Oakland Bay Bridge, in the foreground, crosses from downtown San Francisco to Oakland and is jointed midway at Yerba Buena Island by a tunnel of massive dimensions.

Previous pages: (left) the Embarcadero Center complex. Sidney Walton Park (right) is the village green for the Golden Gateway Center, a planned residential community of apartment towers and condominium townhouses adjacent to San Francisco's financial district. The 1,500-acre Presidio of San Francisco (above), U.S. Sixth Army headquarters, has been a military installation since its establishment by the Spanish in 1776. It encompasses woods, cliffs, beaches, a lake and Old Fort Point, a National Historic site. Facing page: Alcatraz rides the tide 1.25 miles off the San Francisco shoreline in a morning haze, with Bay Bridge in the background. The Rock, phased out as a maximum security prison in 1963, is a popular visitor attraction. The Greco-Romanesque Palace of Fine Arts (overleaf), built for San Francisco's 1915 Panama-Pacific Exposition and restored in 1967, rises out of a lagoon in the Marina District. At right are the Marina Green and St. Francis Yacht Club; at left, Crissy Field, part of the Presidio of San Francisco. In the background, Golden Gate Bridge stretches toward Marin Headlands.

67

Previous pages: (left) San Francisco's Marina district was a fairground during the 1915 Panama-Pacific Exposition. The fair's sole survivor, the Palace of Fine Arts (foreground), was restored in 1967. The boat berths at left belong to the St. Francis Yacht Club. The Embarcadero freeway (right), which covers a stretch of the city's waterfront, was never completed because citizens found it unsightly. The Ferry Building and ferry terminal decks lie on the right, and the Embarcadero Center and Golden Gateway developments on the left, with Telegraph Hill and Alcatraz in the background. Above: the westward view from San Francisco's Richmond and Western Addition districts. The University of San Francisco stands in the left foreground, and the crosstown arterials on the right are Golden Gate Avenue and McAllister Street. The completion of the flat-roofed Moscone Convention Center (facing page) in 1981 has revitalized San Francisco's South of Market district. The razed area at left will become 24-acre Yerba Buena Gardens development. At right, James Lick Freeway leads onto Bay Bridge, which tunnels through Yerba Buena Island. The campanile of the University of California at Berkeley is visible upper right. Overleaf: Nob Hill, with Fairmont and Mark Hopkins hotels in the right foreground and a view east over the financial district to Bay Bridge.

Previous pages: (left) motorists approaching San Francisco via the Bay Bridge are treated to a sweeping view of the city's eastern profile. The clock tower at center is the 1903 Ferry Building, and the white column at right is Telegraph Hill's Coit Tower. Right: San Francisco's Market Street, reaching west from the Ferry Building to Twin Peaks. In the foreground are the Embarcadero Freeway and Justin Herman Plaza with its walk-through Vaillancourt Fountain. To the right of Market Street are the slender towers of the Embarcadero Center, which embraces the wedge-shaped Hyatt Regency Hotel. Facing page: San Francisco's main stem, Market Street (center right) extends from the foot of Twin Peaks to the Embarcadero. City Hall (left), with a dome taller than the national Capitol's, is surrounded by the Davies Symphony Hall, War Memorial Opera House, Federal and State Office Buildings, the Public Library and Civic Auditorium. California Palace of the Legion of Honor (above), a replica of its Paris namesake, occupies a dramatic oceanside site in Lincoln Park near Lands End. Beyond and to the left lies Fort Miley, a U.S. Veterans Hospital. Overleaf: looking east from San Francisco's Van Ness corridor, the panorama takes in, from the left, Telegraph Hill's Coit Tower, Treasure Island Navy base, the downtown skyline, Bay Bridge, Yerba Buena Island and the East Bay communities of Berkeley, Oakland and Alameda.

Facing page: summer fog veils the Golden Gate Bridge, looking northeast towards Raccoon Strait, which separates the Marin County community of Belvedere and Angel Island State Park.
Above: San Francisco's Broadway tunnels through Russian Hill at right, and the Embarcadero Freeway links the waterfront with Broadway. Golden Gateway Commons, real brick townhouses, stand center foreground and Nob Hill lies upper left. Overleaf: (left) looking east from San Francisco's Van Ness corridor toward Nob Hill (left center), shopping district (right center) and financial district, with Bay Bridge, Oakland and Alameda in background. (Right) boat marinas flank Pier 39, with its shopping-restaurant-entertainment complex. To the west are Fisherman's Wharf, the curved pier of Aquatic Park, Marina district and Golden Gate Bridge, while Alcatraz lies far right.

Above: Alcatraz, and, in the background from left, Oakland Bay Bridge, San Francisco's financial district, Fisherman's Wharf and Aquatic Park. Facing page: San Francisco's Embarcadero, with the financial district on the left, and Telegraph Hill, capped by Coit Tower, and Alcatraz in the background. Overleaf: Columbus Avenue cuts through San Francisco's predominantly Italian North Beach from Fisherman's Wharf to the financial district. The triangular skyscraper is the Transamerica Pyramid.